MW00979302

Head Full of Sun

Head
Full of Sun

by Carla Funk

Nightwood Editions
Roberts Creek
2002

Copyright © by Carla Funk, 2002.

All rights reserved. No part of this publication may be reproduced, stored in a retrieval system or transmitted, in any form or by any means, without prior permission of the publisher or, in case of photocopying or other reprographic copying, a licence from CANCOPY (Canadian Reprography Collective), 214 King Street West, Toronto, Ontario M5H 3S6.

We gratefully acknowledge the support of the Canada Council for the Arts and the British Columbia Arts Council for our publishing program.

THE CANADA COUNCIL FOR THE ARTS SINCE 1957 | LE CONSEIL DES ARTS DU CANADA DEPUIS 1957

Cover painting "Above and Below" by Jonathan Puls
Author photograph by Lance Hesketh
Edited for the house by Silas White

National Library of Canada Cataloguing in Publication Data

Funk, Carla
  Head full of sun

Poems.
ISBN 0-88971-185-2

I. Title.
PS8561.U8877H42 2002   C811'.54   C2002-910267-7
PR9199.3.F855H42 2002

Contents

In the Gallery Apocalypse

Tongues of Men and Angels

Darkness Like Dresses

Eve

In the beginning I walked
the garden   clay-stained feet and hair
like a wild thicket   evening fell
warm as breath over us
we slept in the deep
grass until the sound of peacocks
and morning wash of light
then he'd reach his hand
across me and pull a meal
from the leaves   grapes
the size of fists and plums
that split their sweetness
at the tongue's first lick

every day a new invention
fish that leapt silver from the lake
beetles whose wings lifted them
from the ground   then the air
a starry cloud of flowers
my lover's hands naming places
inside me so his flesh and mine
made no difference
overhead the sky swam
in pictures through the dark

some stories refuse to be lost
that serpent scything like a fluid blade

of green through the garden   its voice
dropping the seed in my ear
and the swollen rush of pleasure
in a simple mouthful

some nights I taste it
in my lover's skin   think desire
isn't what it used to be

here at the garden's edge
mosquitoes swarm our sleeping
and his hands hurt   earth-broken
from a day in the dirt   what is there
to say through the long black stillness?
I'm lonely for the sound of
my maker walking the garden
his footsteps half windrush   half
pawprint   and we've become so small
his thumb could sink us

now something stretched like an animal's
skin divides us   a covering and the far-off
hush   always that angel slicing at our backs
the rise and fall of his flaming sword
a wilderness of thorns between us

Goliath's Wife

A day of women hanging
out the tunics of their men   blood
stains whitening in the harsh sun
like battle flags at rest somewhere
the invisible soldiers sleep naked
in the river while the wives wash
and wash the dark stains of their men

home on a trestle of tamaracks
they carried him   the bulk and burden
worth two days' journey
I met them at the well with jugs of water
and though his head now stared
from the tip of a Judean spear
his helmet and shield melted
and hammered into holiness
I knew him still   as if
his limbs wore eyes   the brute
hairy arms and tree-trunk legs
fighting their way back to me

his body laid out like mornings
in the high-roofed house
when I slipped early from his side
to steep juniper tea and slice breadfruit
carry them on a flat stone and set them
on his broad table of a chest

so much of him said the village men
he should have many wives   but he refused
and lifted me above the others
his hands around my waist
like a belt of flesh and bone

alone tonight I'll dream the times
he lifted me to the acacia palm
then stood beside me to name star patterns
pricked into the night
see the hunter with his spear sharpened
to a glittered point   a scattering
of bone dust all around   see this one
like the stream   this one like the bowl
you dip into the well bucket   this one
your hand on my back   this one a woman
wrapped in a man   oh how the cloak
of his love would surround me

across three streams and one cool river
and over the dry forest dust   outside
the quiet tent of a boy smaller than myself
drips my warrior's tired head   the welt
on his forehead the purple thumbprint
of some god who reaches down
to guide the thrown stone

oh that he would lie with me
in this house of high windows
tall doorways   a mammoth bed
too cold these nights alone
that he would mend my burnt-out sky
tend my deepest wound
that the hand of this god
would own me

Rahab

Stories whispered over dark tables
in worried houses
of a God whose hands
melt the hills like wax

the whole city a tremor of fear
for we remembered the Red Sea split
forty years ago like an incision in the land

those evenings
sunsets hung fire
over our heads
and smoke at our feet
from the horizon army camps

and me in the wall of that city
with two men roof-hidden
under sheaves of flax
while the king's messengers searched
my home for spies

and me with their promise
the length of a scarlet rope
a long finger dipped in blood
to mark my window
from the others

the day the wall fell to dust
and the trumpets sounded
a chorus of shouts
the day my Jericho burned
to a heap of ash and stone
another story begins

in another place the builder
reaches down to clear away
a mess of rubble
the thousand fingerprints of men
reaches down
to smooth the ground
begin again

Ruth

I follow behind them
in the field my footprints
in his pressed into the soil
outline of a seed
growing in its shell

this is how I survive
glean what he leaves me
the bread in my mouth
the pattern of his feet

with each bite and swallow
I learn by heart
the progression of toes
arch and tenderness of soles

he spends all night
on the stone threshing floor
winnowing grain from the chaff
midnight when he unrolls his bed
on the ground

outside the door I wait
until he falls asleep
then slip inside
uncover his feet
and find the moon

barley dust between the toes
crescent-shaped calluses
along the heels
this is what has drawn me
across the village
in the middle of night

thin ripples of skin
on the bottoms
when the toes are curled
turquoise veins
written on his feet
like a message

❋

in the middle of the wheat field
he asks me to marry him
gives me his sandals as his pledge
barefoot for the rest of his life
this is what I have dreamed
footprints in the freshly tilled earth
like a map to mark my way home
the warmth of feet upon waking

Bathsheba

These are the rites of cleanliness

two young pigeons sacrificed every month
one for my sins   the other for my impurity

everything I've worn slept on touched
anyone who's touched me must be washed

a clay pot held in unclean hands must be broken
a house with mould on its stones must be torn down
a body with blemish must be atoned for

I unbraid my hair
hold the washcloth
to the inside of my thigh

he can't help but see me
from his rooftop watch me
skin and hyssop   the garden
covered with basins of soapy water
wet sheets hung like banners
on the sycamore branches

and I bathe until he sends for me
my footprints in the wet grass
all the way to his bed

the way newly washed skin calls out
for another body against it
it is impossible to keep clean

✳

In my dreams the child inside me
has the face of a lamb   shiny hooves for hands
I imagine him without a name
small animal designed as offering
even before the fingers are formed
the mouth makes its sound

this birth already a memory
a new cleansing of the womb

the garden   my stained clothes
soaking in sun-warmed water
and my king standing on the palace roof
watching as though he'd never
seen a woman so clean

Jezebel

Stop gravity's pull and the sun's warp
over the morning vineyard   quiet
the page and lay your finger on the verse
where I'm about to look out the window
to my death *(. . . some of her blood*
spattered the wall and the horses
as they trampled her underfoot)
yes   and the dogs licking
for scraps   all slobber and claw
at the exquisite masonry

had I chosen the melon wine
instead of the plate of figs   the dark
boy instead of his fair brother   a ruby
necklace instead of the opal   regret
flexes its handful of burnt fingers
smarts like only yesterday

in this room my life moves like a wall
of running hieroglyphs   saffron eyelids
the blue dust of poppies and lips
pressed purple with the blood of a grape

the resurrected story pushes its ghost
through me to polish up the palace
mirrors   light the throne-room lamps
and smile some happy homecoming

while here in the long and flaring hallways
we women wear our burning
hair and torn eardrums   clutch
this darkness like dresses against
the flame's lick   say over and over
how sorry we've become

Hosea's Wife

Feet cold with the dampness of night half-gone
I slip into our bed and you sound asleep
as though this is how we happen
knowing each other best through absence
and morning when you will kiss
the smell of another on my neck
hold my face to your own like a wound
and say the shameful night has lifted
the day is warm with love

how many times I have ached toward you
only to shift in the presence of men
how to avoid dreams of their mouths lighting on me
and bear the cup of repentance in the house of the Lord
when desire presses its heavy palm against my chest

I leave and return so that the path
between you and everyone else deepens
come back only to feel again
the packed earth under my bare feet
the hands of my lovers growing like fruit under skin
and the succulent voice pulling me out
of our marriage bed into other doorways

sleepwalking hunger like a dark house
and still you wrap me in your love
your arm draped over me in sleep
the always-open window like a hand held out
a promise of food and drink
the ripe harvest and feast

where I have been these lost nights you know
what wet mouths of strangers I have tasted you forgive
like a fig tree in its winter months you wait
while I eat the swollen vineyard

Tamar

Honey   wheat and olives   cracked
barley in the clay bowl of that morning

a shaft of light and the flour dust
suspended mid-air
                              I cannot bake bread
without your mouth on me   you
of the severe kiss and hollow
loving
          how long will your body
like a robe of shadows
hang over me?   how long
will the darkened room
overwhelm?
                    our father
lays his hand to my forehead
as though I am a daughter
for burial   in his house
of worship I am a mourning hymn
the deep slow beat
of a stretched skin drum
                              no wedding
song between these legs   no canopy
or harp   let the sackcloth and ashes be
your thumbprint upon me   scar
to this ever-open wound

Mary Magdalene

I

In the beginning four men stepped through
the glassy coolness of night
took me from the path beside the well
and held me open the way my father used to
stretch the smooth hide of a calf
over flat sun-warmed stones

hunters from a close village they were coming
to this city to buy food for the journey home
it was a long way from where they'd started
and a long way into the night
before I was alone again
and my slippery legs could hold me up

in the end I wanted to crawl into the river
forget how to swim
I wanted Mother to say
something   anything
while she washed the blood
from the insides of my thighs

II

Bursting within me the seeds
split open into a chorus who crooned
their voices with hooked fingers
words like leather straps
pulled tight around my throat
a dark shawl wrapping my face

oh sweet daughter of night
remember the way you freshly let us in
you're made for our kind of love

and Mother cried *what have you done?*
while Father held us screaming on the floor
my voice lost inside all that singing

In the village house where men pressed
their palms against my cheek
and slipped coins under my tongue
in the crowded doorway
where I leaned back humming the hot night
he crouched in front of me
eyes like some faraway sky
he laid his hand on my head
raised from the deep
every ache I'd ever gathered
that one touch
loosening grief's thick knots

I was a child at the well again
holding a corner of my father's shirt

IV

How can I not follow
this man whose body bleeds
love in the city streets

men fall on their faces for his touch
mothers push feverish babes
into his arms
clutch the hem of him
as though holding gold

in the pool at Bethesda
I washed his feet
fed him bread and goat's milk
in the high mountains

through sand-burnt journeys
and multitudes of people
I have carried his wineskin

some nights I lean next to him
over a small fire our palms
held open to the flames

some nights I burn
learning to make this
kind of love
instead of another

V

Now this terrible darkness
my bed and a canopy of stars
the moon and salted night

on the stone window ledge
the shape of a cat moves inside
the blue-black silhouette
of a lone olive tree

of all the gifts he could have given
I'm blessed with visions
that come like a hand over my eyes
his body a trunk of light rising
from the ground then his feet
shot through with stars

every night I'm hearing them
the angels with their damp wings dragging
over the grass they leave
trails of spice and fine oils
myrrh and sandalwood
the scented road rising high above earth
the stones with their flat tongues
of dust crying out

An Alphabet of Psalms

Psalm of Assumptions

The man with the close-cropped cap of hair
wears his T-shirt like a banner
"God is dead" –Nietzsche
"Nietzsche is dead" –God
you know this kind of man   his religion
like a brand name   holiness a logo

assume at night he sleeps sound
as Christ in the boat's belly
and drives a car with a silver fish
glued to the bumper

and he's simple with philosophy
reads the Bible and ultra-right-wing publications
for fun   porch-kissed a girl once
but not before repentance for the worm
that crawled up his pant leg
in the starry twilight musk

his heart pumps a cliché factory
of proverbs and spiritual maxims
his head a refrigerator door
magnetic for vague platitudes

> *The best things in life aren't things*
> *Commit random acts of kindness*
> *Smile   Jesus loves you*

his childhood smells like Betty Crocker
casseroles church potlucks his mother apron-clad
sings in the choir and his father kisses her cheek
every evening upon his *honey-I'm-home* arrival

his faith moves an escalator beneath him
a blind pull up to a higher floor
where everything's the same as down here
and his God built of need and shame
clay and spit erodes with the flood
that history writes itself a false start
that double-minded men love the law

assume the night that presses him down
into bed and the face at the window
whose look cuts glass is all his own
a making that sings in doubt   undoes the soul

Psalm of the Bedroom Floor, 1991

Bureau mirror and fake wood panelling
and grey electrical box above my bed
the glass lamp with its hot bulb dying
a window that slides open the scent
of night stalk vanilla and damp earth
through the screen

I'm on my knees again
face and hands flat on the carpet

above me the kitchen floor
and my father's late-night shuffle
for a cold glass of milk
as he manoeuvres the dark

down here   mercy
has never been the issue

repentance   on the other hand

I've no rosary to slip bead by bead
no abacus for my sins
but the soul has its own mathematics
and a ghost hand that scrawls
the empty chalkboard

tonight the equation leans

heavy on this side of my head
and forgiveness that soothes
the dark like a mother's hand
over a fevered forehead
plays hard to find

I've got the word iniquity stuck
in my skin   a mosquito's sting
that won't quit and a tall boy's
arms that pull me down with wanting

somewhere in my heavy Bible
there is a verse underlined in blue
that upholds the virtue of the pure
something about the chaste
I'm trying to understand

Psalm of 'Carla'

Take my name and its meaning
(*strong and womanly*) take me
bone and tooth   blood and nail
take the scar on my forehead
and the incision in my belly
take my weak music and empty pockets
unfinished sentences that stutter
toward wholeness

erase the soundscape of telephone voices
calling *Carla* and the mouth of one particular boy
wet your thumb and rub out the harsh syllables
the hard 'C' and adolescent insecurity
like a fishing hook through the lip

stitch rip the homemade dresses of childhood
with hand-sewn labels and Christmas gift tags
birthday cards and a caricature
of me pushing a doll carriage
drawn by a Maui beach artist

let your hand scoop deep
into the bed of marrow
begin again   zygote
to your mercy   nameless
to your flame

Psalm of Deepest Night

for my mother

Bedside this last night you stay
to rub your youngest sister's back
hold a glass of water to her mouth
though she can no longer swallow
and even the tiny white tablets
of morphine are stones on her tongue

the whole room full of her sound
each breath like a weak bow pulled across
a cello's loosened strings
and the square clock pushing
its hands through the dark

and though you haven't been to church in years
you sing every hymn remembered
from the small sanctuary of childhood

(McMinnville Oregon
back seat of a blue station wagon
eight children with ice cream cones
after a long Sunday service)

a slide show in your head
as you turn and turn
the gold ring loose on her
blue-tipped finger
the oxygen leaking
from her blood

feeling in this house of darkness
a pair of hands tying night's
weary cape around you
as you dip and wring out
the cloth in the silver basin
hold it cool to your sister's forehead

seeing in this deepest part of night
you don't belong   visitor to this place
carved out by sickness while her body
spans the threshold between heaven
and earth   as though Jesus sits on the edge
of this bed too   waits as she pauses
once more in the doorway
for that final look around these rooms
a woman checking lights out
windows locked and oven off
not wanting to forget a thing
in the coma's heavy veil you brush against
when your hand moves
the damp cloth to her lips

and like a child reaching
down into a wishing pool
you're shoulder-deep in the dark
blood of night   plumbing the depths
for that single coin of light

Psalm of Easter Break Vacation, 1981

In the fibreglass hemlock forest my father
stands amazed as though he's come upon
a mythic realm whose language stuns the air
Similkameen   glacier   sasquatch   Bella Coola
each word a huge hand of cold
touching the landscape

he who buys his hunting licence every fall
but cannot bring himself to pull the trigger
finds in this wilderness gallery
the miracle of resurrection
though he wouldn't know to call it that
just a bunch a dead animals brought back

synthetic bats strung mid-flight
by an empty cave's entrance
a lithe cougar set to strike
the bighorn ram caught eternally
on the somewhat realistic bluff

he touches the glass eye of a deer
and expects the animal to bolt

to coax a bear's body out of its flat hide
to place each fish back in the stream
with the precision of one who knows them
to reassemble the ornate bonework of a bird

these things he could imagine
himself doing well
in the way a maker shapes his world
out of stick and mud and sweat

gathers the beautiful useless
off the highway's shoulder
and calls it alive
calls it good

Psalm of Falling

Midnight oil and the long necks of streetlamps
hitched to the concrete
                              I'm here in the flesh
but the heart floats without a string
                                        I know
a man's hands can make the dark swell
and flame at the wick
                        or so I'm told
by other girls whose stories began
in the more confident rooms of love

Julia tells us a lover waits for her in Mexico
on a fishing boat his nets alive with dorado
and tuna
            surely he keeps a small house lit
with lanterns in the evening and a hammock
tied to his porch
                    surely he swims inside
her head like a pet fish and certain angles
of glass make him appear larger than reality

and Angie pulls a Polaroid of a high school boy
from her boot like it's the winning ticket

but me
      I've got my own backroom story
a knocked-off father-daughter plot that plays
this sidewalk like a stuck melody
                           (take it downstairs
down to the basement down to the floor
down to the bone)
                there's a man
who drives his Buick Skylark
past this corner every Tuesday lunch
rolls down his window a crack more each week
I imagine he's caving to the skin
like all of us
             that a piece of him holds the edge
like a climber to a cliff
                 where once you let go
all that you remember is the fall

Psalm of Galileo

True the moon wears mountains
like the pale shoulders of a sleeping girl
the Milky Way swims
with schools of stars
and Jupiter spins like a juggler
around the sun

true my scope can settle the distance
between this weighted earth
and flash of galaxies
I can witness Venus flex
her light and dark
the planets turn from night to night

but where is the measure of faith
I need to slit heaven's underbelly
peel back the holiness
a difficult birth

like the frozen particles of breath
that hover in this winter night
so the remnants of his speech hang
banners over me

by blade of grass or ounce
by span of wing or pound of flesh
what length or height or breadth
can calculate the divine
in a string of numbers
on parchment my quill tip
dry and bent with trying

Psalm of Honesty

Late November and the bare-branched
apple trees beside the highway
bear what little fruit remains
each apple one red word
against the blank page of sky
a parable in this worn-out orchard
how it hurts to take everything off
stand naked at the foot of the bed
the foot of the cross

long Sundays in the Mennonite church
I'd hold my father's hand in my lap
peel back his palm's tough calluses
each yellow thread of skin exposing
the new skin beneath
while at the front of the sanctuary
other sinners poured out
testimonies into the microphone
each confession a tender lash of grace
drawing them deeper into the holy of holies

how to redeem the lost art of repentance
separate the penance from the sin
so that when I say *I'm sorry*
I don't wear the words for days
like coat upon coat upon heavy coat

how to lay it down
in the throne room
where words undress the voice
unbutton me to the bone
so the heart hangs
in the white space
like the apple left
on its leafless tree in fall
a pathetic resilience and surrender

Psalm of Infertility

Last night the dream of
an egg to my ear
and its slow black heart
ripples through
the translucent shell

I crack it open
remove a small boy
no bigger than my thumb
and hold him
to the kitchen light
as though to candle
the tiny yolk of his pulse

seven years since
I pushed out my daughter
and nothing more

many months of waiting
doctor's visits
the removal of what
medical texts so sumptuously
call *chocolate cysts*

tonight I listen
to the laughter of Sarah
with her desert womb
to Hannah's prayer
on the floor of the mountain temple
her dry breasts like silent tongues

wait for the God of healing
to dip his hand in this spit and clay
and from a wound   shape a garden

Psalm of July 1978,
Photograph

I'm clinging to your knees
on the edge of Paddle Lake
the aluminum boat glinting
and our feet deep
in the stiff shore-grass

crumpled face and tears
at your leaving
I'm saying
take me with you
I want to climb inside
your orange life jacket

and Mother with her camera eye
sees you and I like a brief flash of fin
leaping from water

a fish licking the air with its whole body
to taste the new element of pain

Psalm of Kisses

We're in the garden again with dusk
owlsong   the sky lit with star maps
and Eve's mouth   a thin slice
of fruit between her teeth
Adam lured to her lips   hungry
for that first kiss   desire
slipping history the tongue

First kiss behind the woodshed
where Father's cigarette butts
make a wide ring
around the chopping block
that boy's mouth wet
and tasting like salt
and vinegar potato chips
the rest of our friends
throwing snowballs in the trees

Second kiss a midnight game
of hide and seek in the subdivision's
unfinished houses   he and I crouch
in the bones of someone's future
bedroom or shower stall
our hands on each other's faces

✸

Third fourth fifth and sixth kisses
all those Christmas dances
in the small auditorium
where I bribe friends to catch me
in slow dances with the boy
of that season's longing
hold the plastic mistletoe above us
while dry ice haunts the strobe-lit dark
and speakers shake the floor
all of us caught us in lust's musky fog

✸

Dangerous seventh kiss in the hot tub
with the Swiss exchange student
who plays trumpet and whose lips
improvise jazz riffs over my neck
summer sky black and stellar
I sink with his hands around my thighs

✳

My room of married kisses
to which I close the door
and turn the key
as though some vow
would break were I to spill
my husband's soft
lips in the throw of things
in that dark
and lovely garden

✳

And all those kisses in between
that fall into memory's junk drawer
of lost keys half-burnt candles greeting
cards old telephone numbers blunt
scissors rat traps crazy glue a length
of rope dead batteries a deck of
playing cards a lock for which you'll never
remember the combination
all those kisses you'd rather forget

Psalm for the Lover

I have a lover
whose body
smells of spikenard and myrrh
the ground bulb of an orchid
the planed flesh of a tree

in the dark basement
of my need   he undresses
every inch of me
and I'm Lazarus
to his loving

Psalm of Mercy

Don't tell her my mother half begs
how this morning my father found the tomcat
on the lawn pawing at a sparrow
until its tail feathers lay in a heap

oh he swatted that cat good my mother said
and couldn't bear the bird without flight
so set it on the gravel
brought his work boot down

and I want to tell my daughter
who still holds this man up
to a certain level of goodness

I was her age once
six years old and watching
through the kitchen window
as my father in the white driveway
brought the blunt back
of the shovel down
on our dog's head as she lay pinned
beneath the wheel
of the neighbour lady's low-bed truck

my mother's soapy hands
half covering my eyes
her wet apron cold against my back

at the edge of the property my father
chopped a hole in the frozen lagoon
slipped the dog through the green stench

I watched from behind the woodshed
threw a chunk of ice at him
when he turned his back
missed by an inch

later at supper he pushed away his plate
shook his head at me
I had to do it his explanation
worth nothing then and reason
enough to dream a bigger shovel
coming down on him that night

twenty years later my head's version
of my father carries with it that moment
the grey morning heavy with wet snow
the low-bed jackknifed in the driveway
the sharp rise and fall of the shovel
bearing down on the dog's skull

what I've come to expect
from my father   a philosophy of mercy
that wears skin and sheds blood
hurts for all its rawness
mercy that brings the heart doubling
back for more

Psalm of Need

What you don't know
hurts you now   the cramping after-
clots dripping from you
so that your young head swims
upon standing   you grab the
counter edge   steady   see
the bathroom mirror cut you in half
at the waist   your belly a mess
of pain
            when your mother gets home
from groceries   lugs the sacks inside
the front door and hollers your name
come help me with this stuff
you're calling out the same words but they're
deeper   down the dark whirlpool
sucking you under   down on the floor

later at the hospital when the white gloves
of doctors have lifted   and your body
surfaces like a child who's been held under-
water too long   your mother won't look at you
she bends the flexible straw to your mouth
and you swallow
                  call this moment *shame*
you burning under these stiff sheets
because you had no idea   your mother
searching her purse for a hairbrush   Aspirin

something
             the slow hemorrhage
of the heart starts here pouring out loss
into an empty house   and what you don't know
still holds you   bleeds into the many rooms
of your need   a steady hand
washing down the wound

Psalm of the Obvious

Sometimes the stories arrive so bluntly
you think they're lies   like the one about
the diver whose soul split open the dark
how every scripture each gospel word
his friend told again and again like a stuck record
finally spilled to overflowing
at the edge of the platform

he was the only one in the building
that late night   hadn't bothered
to turn on the lights

his silhouette on the aquatic centre's wall
combined with the moon's stark
beam through the glass ceiling
made as he stood backward
with arms outstretched for a simple fall-in
a rippled cross

he sat on the tower's edge
thirty feet up and settled his aches
with God   traded emptiness for blood

so that when the night-shift janitor
turned on the fluorescent lights
and lit the empty pool bottom
drained earlier that day for repairs
there was meaning in the moment
in the quickened pulse and dark

Psalm of Peru
for Roberta

There's a God you say because you were thirteen
swimming in Peru and the ocean's
undercurrent pinned you to the floor
floating warm on the bottom
you heard your heart from the inside out
a slow throb against the rib-cage
surprised at drowning's tenderness
and persuasion like the huge hand
of a lover pressing you down

then the voice in your ear clear and stern
as a parent saying *come here* or *get up*
and you obeyed just as a person knows to
blink at the suddenness of light
you knew to kick to the surface
your legs pushed up and up until your arms
felt another's arms and hands grasp you

when your head crowned the first thing
you saw was a small cross   a flash of gold
nailing sunlight to the barrel-chested man
who heaved you over his hairy shoulder
laid you on the beach then his mouth over yours
and the taste of sea in your throat

later on the sand your mother and father
and older sisters stood over you
and rubbed your shoulders with towels
pushed wet ropes of hair from your face
and you gasped to explain it all
the underwater voice and gold-cross man
the invisible weight of him who carried you up
imaginary they said *some water mirage*
a long blink on the verge of unconsciousness

as with gravity and plate tectonics and the Peruvian ruins
you photographed with a Polaroid camera
the pictures sliding out clear and now
clouded film blooming into evidence of things seen
so too with this imaginary saviour
some angel who slipped into the costume of a man
so too with the lifeguard god no one else saw
you have proof in the turquoise vein
in the blood and beat of it

Psalm of Questions

I cry out to you, O God,
but you do not answer . . .
—Job

While the morning stars sang
and angels dipped low their buckets
in the sea of glass
where were you

who shut this cupboard of sea
when it poured forth whitewater
and a gushing womb

who sealed the sky
with a wax thumbprint
when the flood overwhelmed

have you shown twilight the back door
like a lover ushered out
plucked moon and stars
like apples or set the sun spinning
a child's top for outer space

do you know how
corner to corner the earth fits
a folded sheet shaken loose
of blood and hunger

have you opened storehouses
of snow where the white fist
cold aches itself earthward
or unlocked the lightning
room below

can you string Pleiades
on a silver chain or loosen
Orion's starry cord
call up constellations
like a shepherd to his flock

of heaven's water jars and raven's wing
of salt flats and stork eggs
of fishhook and leviathan
who carries wisdom's cup

whose beginning wraps the darkness
and whose end bursts a fire
whose nothing fills the broken
bowl to overflow

whose wound heals wounded
sweet balm to the deep incision

whose questions come like answers
to the spirit's inner ear

Psalm of Regret

In this script I write you capable
of untying your bootlaces
though your hands are cracked with cold
your eyes heavy with rum

I write you steady on the staircase
though your legs buckle
like a child's on ice skates for the first time

I build the room full of words
and these words tender
yes and *that's all right* and *I know*

I bring you a cold glass of milk
without being asked

I say things you might want to hear
like *this morning I saw two deer*
in the white field across the road
or *remember the fried trout at Mud Lake*

in this choreography of regret
I'll fix the moment like a stage
with better props and gestures
and take you in my arms
the way a different daughter might

Psalm of Shoes

True windows into a man's deepest parts
they offer the gift of discernment
to any woman who takes the time
to look through them

my friend Sindee swears she can look back
on all her past loves and see them
for what they really were
by their shoes
the one wearing high-tops
with laces perpetually loose
oozed laziness   his sloppy heart
losing everything she ever gave him
and the sockless one in white leather deck shoes
complete with fringe and tassels
turned out to be strictly ornamental

and stay away she said from any guy
whose shoes reek of manure
though he's easy to find in a room full of people
poor hygiene only works its way up
the shoes infectious

the punctuation of a man's wardrobe
shoes set the tone decide the syntactical
impossibilities of romance

take for example cowboy boots
the pointy exclamations of footwear
the *yee-haw* and *howdy* of the overeager
you know his keenness to please
will wear thin as his worn buckskin toes

and brown leather hikers like the semicolons
who show their versatility   half comma   half period
I can be anything you want me to be
sensitive dangerous just tell what you want

or the Birkenstock sandals whose ellipses insist
the cultured heart lives here
I know Wagner and Nietzsche and the imagist movement . . .
it's sometimes hard not to be impressed

a warning though
watch out for imitations
those fake suede look-alikes
bought under the fluorescent lights
of chain department stores

these are the "quotation marks" of men's footwear
how easily the weak seams of their synthetic
hearts rupture   never lasting
as long as the real thing

sometimes your best bet is no shoes at all
the barefoot men of beaches
hippie communes
lazy suburban backyards

but when you meet the man
whose shoes overwhelm you
my advice to you is this
invite him out to a restaurant café   whatever
and before your breathless dialogue begins
ask him to please remove his shoes
right there in the middle of the room
in front of you and everyone

if without a blink of hesitation
he takes his shoes off   you'll know
he's more than just his pair
of classic-yet-rugged Oxfords
with stitching detail
but if he feigns disbelief at your request
makes a poor excuse about
foot odour   dirty socks
has that unmistakable look
of an animal caught in your high beams
you'll know   it's obvious
inside those shoes
he's got something to hide

Psalm of Thirst

The sun like a burning eye stares
until the river shrivels into lines
and all that remains of the rainy season
is a watering hole sludged with elephant dung
the air a banner of gnats and tsetse flies

as the deer longs for water
so much more the creatures of this place
who bear the blueprint of thirst
in their bone-dry bellies

in this open throat of dry land
the island blends into the plain
and grown pelicans nesting there
begin to leave in search of water
while the young flightless ones left behind
walk over the cracked clay for days
until their charcoal bodies give out
fleck the baked landscape
in small feathered heaps

❋

I'm thirsty the man says
in the early morning heat on the hill
the first rays of sun swelling the horizon

in his mouth the weight of a whole earth
a thick coat of dust lining his throat

to his lips the hyssop branch
soaked with gall   that final drink
swallowing all the light from this place

❋

As deep calls to deep
in the immeasurable electricity of God
so thirst calls to water
the dry-tongued stones licking
the morning air   desperate
a man stumbling across
the sun-scorched sand
the word *oasis* a cold pool
of hope in his mouth

so the porous heart soaks up
what rain and goodness he sends

so my deserts turn to gardens
in the presence of the Lord

Psalm of Us

We've been trying
we tell friends and family
who ask when our time will come
when my belly will once again bloom
that taut honeydew fullness

and we have been trying –
vitamins A through E
meticulously charted body temperatures
the coming and coming together

our doctor's suggestion to get away
has brought us now to my childhood home
split-level in a small town
miles from everywhere

we spend days with relatives eating pie
and walk the river trails
I cleared six years ago for a summer job
play cribbage on my parent's front lawn
fifteen two fifteen four and a pair is six
trying at laziness before night
comes furtive over us

and we bathe brush our teeth
scent our necks with whatever
drives fantasies into the open
crawl under the hand-stitched quilt
in the bedroom of my adolescence

despite the green shag rug and the whir
of my mother's sewing machine across the hall
we feel our way toward each other

get saturated the doctor says
when ovulation is imminent
so we come together quietly
evening upon evening
in the occupation of desire

my head flashing photographs
from every pregnancy book I've ever read
graphic pictures of slick heads crowning
heavy-breasted women who hold the undersides
of their stretched bellies
serenity bursting at the seams
the pressure builds nightly   monthly

visualize the union of egg and sperm
one book urges with precise ink
drawings of reproductive combustion
as though imagery can wish itself
into being   the empty cup
suddenly overflowing with wine
and two dry sticks rubbed together
pushing a single spark of light
through the room's swollen dark

Psalm of Veils

This morning a heavy veil of clouds
and certain rain
the kind of day that stands
a child at the door's threshold
staying in   wanting out

the door is two doors
and I'm the child
a girl of five in dress and tights
alone in the foyer
of the Mennonite church

here's where the preacher stands
to shake our Sunday hands goodbye
after the sermon and long slough of hymns

here are the coat racks and steep steps up
to the balcony of high windows
their yellow glass shining sun on us
no matter what the weather outside

II

During Wednesday morning ladies' Bible study
my mother fervent in the basement prayer huddle

I'd roam the empty sanctuary upstairs
bright orange pews polished to a slide
green hymnals tucked symmetrical in slots
tiny pencils sharpened to perfect points
next to the white collection envelopes

and sometimes with all the fluorescent lights off
I'd sneak behind the pulpit
slip my hand inside the velvet offering bags
to check for lost coins
or try on a pair of the pastor's
black-rimmed reading glasses
feeling the whole time a measure of guilt
as if I'd stepped over some invisible line
in the house of the Lord

III

And I'm thinking of the high priest
on the Day of Atonement
with his sacred linen sash
and bowl of smoking incense
bending down to double-knot
the length of rope around his ankle
before he'd slip behind the elaborate curtain
enter that most holy place

fear that the censer's cloud couldn't cover him
that he might see the blazing face of God
need to be pulled out by the other priests
reeled hand over hand from altar's burning

In one story the spirit gives itself up
a cry loud enough to split rock
quake the ground

in another the final breath of Jesus
rises in the shape of two hands
to tear the temple veil top to bottom

a heap of burnt cloth and
everything old falls
lays down its garments
sheds its final skin

Psalm of Water

For the baby whose head weeps
fluid in the womb and his mother
what comfort
and into what pool of grief
did your hand dip in the making

she comes home from the hospital
with a bouquet of white roses
and a stack of cursive sympathy
cards signed *our prayers are with you*
what consolation
when night slides the half-shaped
face of her child into Valium dreams
two parts hydrogen and one part air

three weeks later on an empty beach
she sings with her husband
and a small group of friends
of your *sweet sweet mercy*
two parts body and one part blood
reads the gospel passage
of the woman at the well

no irony lost here
in your offer of living water
a handful enough to heal
the deepest wound
or flood the empty womb

Psalm of 'X'

Great unknown   author of moon
and burning seas   the hollow chambers
of the heart   touch your healing hand
to the small of my back and take my pain
like a rocket to your throne

set down the flaming sword
and minister to my need as a man
in the throb and glow of night
holds his lover   tender with purpose

when the blanket dusk falls over my eyes
such a shipwrecked dark   be the shore
of bright phosphorescence   shine a green
womb about my burnt-out soul

when the sand grows hands
that sink me deep   swing down
your heavenly rope

wash me in the shadow
of your glory   call me naked
to your arms and I'll trade
shame for a cup of water
a cup of water
for a mouthful of wine

unknowable and unknown
let me know you
like a nail through your palm
a hand through your gaping side
let me know you skin
and let me know you blood

in the dense and heavy wilderness
let me find you compass
to my wandering   answer
to my fallen question

Psalm of Years Later

The uphill walk and trying
not to appear out of breath
as we rounded the road to his house
cutting school with a dread and anticipation
knowing I'd be kissed a little
more than I wanted
in his dark basement

how to repent the lost decade
unmake my head's stubborn movies
in which boy and girl sit forever on the edge
of the unmade bed wanting
to lie down under the pretense of exhaustion
wondering who should make that first move
and when that first move has been made
how to unmake it

take into that girl's arms
the young boy who tried to take her
in the downstairs bedroom ten years ago
while a soap opera flickered mute
in the television set by her head
wanting to pull them close
the way a mother might urge her two belligerent
children together into the same room
to resolve their quarrelling
believing in the law of proximity –
closeness eventually yields forgiveness

inhale the thin filaments of smoke
that film her hair later as she lights her first
and only cigarette on his front lawn
while on the porch the boy's mother
pours a round of rum
as though mothers do this sort of thing
for their children

the clink of glass on glass
a cut stone of sound she'll hear
ten years later when it doesn't matter anymore
when his mother is dead from a car accident
and he is a man with a wife
a small child and night shifts at the mill

break the surface of the brain's pool
with a casual thought of him
though it makes no difference
how he thinks of me – that girl
I want to take by the shoulders
and shake for aching too much
over the ones who didn't matter
to whom she didn't matter

Psalm of Zion

Explain to me how the body falls asleep
synapse by synapse and cell by cell
lies down quiets down to hush mode
the heart's slow marathon toward dying
and the final breath a broken ribbon
that breathes *we're home*

in my head the crystalline sidewalks
beam apostles and floating relatives
Aunt Linda encounters the wife of Jonah
beside a glass sea full of whales
blowing silver waterspouts
or my great-grandfather of
the high-backed wheelchair
crouches down to speak
to a small boy burnt once
in Herod's fires
now whole again

explain to me the body as a seed
sown deep in the ground
how the harvest of skin and bone
defies gravity in the heavenly metropolis
whose traffic is all angels and praise
up the bright highway

explain the difference between
how the head dreams
this many-mansioned place
with picture-book gold streets
and panthers tame for petting
and how the spirit longs
in its lonely dialect
for something more golden and other
than the fathoming head

someplace a girl might crawl
onto the lap of the father and see
her name carved like a destination
in the crease of his palm
and he would rest his hand
upon her head and say
this is beginning
this is end

In the Gallery Apocalypse

Dream Apocalypse

And I heard a great voice out of the temple saying to the seven angels, Go your ways, and pour out the vials of the wrath of God upon the earth.

–Revelation 16:1

FIRST VIAL
sore

What begins as thick red teardrops
hits the skin with acid glow
lesions open bright anemones
boils the size of climbing roses
the whole body a profusion of bloom

like the burn my daughter gave herself
as a baby scooting her high chair
toward the stove so she could reach
the bright element of pain
something magnetic in the blood
her small palm a swirled scar

here in the streets people
raise their useless umbrellas
hold their hands to their faces
while God wrings out the heavens

SECOND VIAL
sea of blood

Somewhere the leeches are dreaming
sucking themselves seaward

as the Egyptians swam in an ocean
of blood   their children dripping dark
puddles on the shore
so the slit arteries of the sea
pour out and the wine-coloured
sky soaks up the deep

in the final movement of the red song
whales burst geysers of blood
from the tops of their slippery heads
eels slice blindly through the murky bottoms
and the sharks drink in
the heaviness of their frenzy

rivers, fountains of blood

To the one still searching for that
youth fountain in the lush
jungle of myth

come here
to where a bright spring
surges the very
drink of life

how different
the story of Narcissus
had he stared into this
river of blood

a mirror of the flesh
turned inside out

burning sun

From every poet a version of Icarus
flying too close to the sun
wax wings dripping down his back

now this
the sun flying too
close to us   a hot fist
bearing down
so that houses slow-melt
like chunks of ice
into vast suburban puddles

the neighbourhood a canvas
that weeps   colours smeared
like the messy handprints
of children over fresh walls

the night's collective dream
tunnels through fever
and burning bedclothes
into the high blue air
sleepwalks the winter snowscape
while the body's quicksilver rises
flickers its thin tongue of fire

FIFTH VIAL
darkness

You're standing in a parking lot
among rows and rows of cars
when it comes

the sudden fireworks
of electrical outages
blades of coloured glass
filling the black bolt
of unrolled sky

had you a flashlight
a box of emergency candles
a matchstick or lantern
you'd consider this *beautiful*
in the way some museum paintings
hang themselves in the mind
even after the tour is over

but now it's a set of keys
an endless sense of touch you need
not to mention a brilliant map home

SIXTH VIAL
dry river

This river has nothing
to do with you   has no place
in your soul's glossy atlas
its skinny goats and cows
bellowing over the dead
banks a globe away

what ghost ships heaved
upon its shores   what women
carried jugs of water
on their fine dark heads
what children dove
in the bottle-green currents
traipsed home
with heads full of sun
mean nothing but postcard
fodder to the camera-eye
full-colour spread
in a travel agent's dream

now even the camels
with their water-bearing humps
hunt down the hot shade
their bodies bone scaffolds
on the verge of collapse
and the river bottom's fossils
breathe toward the surface

finding realism overrated
you'd prefer to sit this trip out
pass time reading the travel guide's
history of city monuments
and hints for a spectacular
romantic getaway in the hills
where the banquet pours on
and the glass in your hand
brims paradise and a full-bodied red

you whose cup runs dry
in other ways lift an empty hand
to your mouth   lick the fingertips'
salt and hold them to the air
a gesture called *thirst* or
anxious tourist in strange weather
a photograph worth capturing
against the dust and thirsty sunset

the voice, the earthquake, the hail

Tonight the city reveals itself
like a body worn through at the skin
streetlamps and windows in full shatter
like a cascade of china poured off
the roof of a thirty-storey building
the sidewalk a dangerous glass maze
only the blind would walk
barefoot   faith being the absence
of things seen and in this case
one's only shining chance

at what?   we want to know
the story's ending split open
like a freshly sutured wound

we can explain the slow rub of plate tectonics
the earth's fiery mantle rising
in the shape of hands to pull
whole islands down like childhood
rafts caught with water

we can explain the geology of a great city
split three ways   *much like a banana*
says the TV seismologist holding up the fruit
in its trinity of natural fault lines

and it's no one's fault really
to trace the gaping continental
holes back to the garden   back to
that burnt-out angel's resignation
borders the absurd

these hailstones the size of fists
that beat our roofs to shingled pulp
and flatten the summer's flowerbeds
to a spread of torn dresses
we can take them too
and trace our days like bruises
turning sunsets of colour
say *we're fine   we're alive aren't we?*

aside from evening that sings the voice
into our sleep   the dust of many galaxies
weight of many veils   that deep cry
coming home   aside from the words
it is finished   hurled headlong into space
and back into the broken bedrooms
where our dreams like echo chambers
make earthquakes of their own

In the Gallery Apocalypse

The sign above the door splashed in red
tells you to take it all off   strip down
to the skin of a child for whom skin
sings like moonlight after bath
the whole golden length of you
dipped in the glowing inkwell of night

your nakedness essential
as stomach to hunger
disorientation to map
the sun's flint and tinder
to the fire's gutted house

forget how to get here   just come
follow the tunnel's steep climb to the place
where the man with the seven-star hand
waits with his bracelet of heavy keys
white bird perched on his head
translator   curator   mediator
who was who is and is to come
it hardly matters now you're here

I. WOMAN WITH DRAGON

Draped with the sun's warp
she shimmers like heat
off a summer highway
her heart a jukebox of slow blues

> *I was a girl once too*
> *broken in the suburbs*
> *mouth full of candy*
> *head full of stars*
> *look how far I've travelled*
> *desert   ocean   mountain   valley*

and she gives like a mirror
the sultry pageant of your own
girlhood   lessons in falling
and the dark bedrooms

press your head to the canvas
hear this painting's undercoat
rush a river of blood and song
for this woman's throaty push
the newborn's flushed lungs
the beast's many mouths set
to swallow galaxies whole

II. LAMB AND SCROLL

Perspective is everything

where you stand to look inside
this frame's perfect circle
will determine the tangent and degree
of your shame

whether you see or do not see
this lamb with its torn throat
standing in the centre of every story

it's all here   the wash of red
over the doorway the garden kiss
and crown of thorns   the hollow tomb
a wilted angel lifting up its bloodshot eyes

take the brush and paint your own
wound in the middle of this scroll
split forehead or cracked spine
the long year of loneliness
welts in the shape of a lover or
father   the tightly sutured heart
spilling at the seams

III. ALPHA/OMEGA

Like Escher whose hands dipped
in the ink of continuous staircases
made his day and night fly black
against white in the woodcut sky
so God of the Greek alphabet
begins and ends eternal
his single strand of light
thread through this screen
a filament of fire
for the skull's dark caves

IV. GREAT MULTITUDE IN WHITE ROBES

They have just stepped across
the threshold and dropped
their bundles of clothing –
pants, dresses, scarves, shoes –
everything into the ivory river

where angels wing-deep in lather
wring the laundry's dirt and shake out
loose robes of rapturous white
the sky's clothesline pinned
with sheets of light

and the freshly dead on the shore's far side
slipping into these second-skins   like guests
dressing for an elaborate wedding   one young girl
bending her neck forward and turning her pale back
to fingers that hook and close the tiny eyes

in this fresco of transformation
even the cells' invisible
amulets sing praise
even the river stones
whitewashed with light
cry out

V. THREE ANGELS

The origami of this
foreground angel
wing-edges folded
like a feathered crane
swims the glassy
throne-room floor

this second angel
aorta of its translucent heart
pumping light as it hangs
from the seam of a cloud
makes a kind of chandelier
the others swim beneath
tongues like wicks
lit with incense

and finally that third
and centre angel
whose whole body
having grown enough sight
to drink in all this glory
blinks a costume of eyes
that pour out colour
like jewels in the palm

this blue the blue of peacock
sky and sapphire
this red the red of cherries
flame and blood

VI. WHITE HORSE WITH RIDER

Remember the neighbour's Appaloosa
sucking sugar cubes from your open palm
then its yellow teeth sinking clean
into your thumb

remember being picked up by your jacket hood
clenched in the mare's bite   thrown ten feet
across the barnyard and Uncle Larry laughing
you're all right   no cracked bones

for this lithograph your fear of horses
melts black to white to a clear calm
as Jesus rides bareback into the barnyard
on his dream-white stallion
where you're lying winded   broken

dismounts and dusts you off
picks the straw from your hair and holds
the stirrup steady while you swing up
and away hanging on for sweet life
as you fly the blazing skyline
your fingers dug deep into his sides

Heaven split open
and each gate swings a pearl
for the dead now awake
as they enter the city
to which all longing returns

and in their procession lay down
at the entrance their husks
of deep sorrow   bodies
peeled down to the new

and like the oyster in its shell
that covers over its pain
a single grain of sand
layer upon layer
so these pearls thicken
with each ache and grief
each lonely bone laid down

on the inside of this iridescent sky
there is a smoothing over   a turning
and turning of the wound
into splendour

Tongues of Men and Angels

Disclaimer

When I say "my father" I might mean
the man who came to the hospital two hours late
peered into the nursery window
and declared me the ugliest baby he'd ever seen
or I might mean the God into whose arms
I want to crawl on those broken
empty-room nights

and when I say "mother"
and the mother says "daughter"
and the daughter sounds a lot like me
any resemblance is purely chance
poetic coincidence

when the mother in the poem says things like
"if you play with your belly button
you'll come untied   zoom wildly
around the room like a deflating balloon
end up a loose sack of flesh on the floor"
neither the poem nor the daughter
quite believes her

when I say "daughter"
I might mean the one I dreamed I'd be
long-legged   narrow-hipped with lips
that pout and smile simultaneously

when I call you beautiful
I might be harbouring resentment

when my hands at the night's bright screen
type out "your hands" there is a certain amount
of longing   sometimes a thousand
handfuls   sometimes more

when I write "evening" I'm usually thinking
a teenager's version of the night   the omniscient
darkness and two kids
all eager mouth and hands
on the living-room floor
until six in the morning
when the girl realizes
she's made a huge mistake
this isn't the kind of guy she'd marry
and it's too late   time doesn't rewind
like the stupid action movie they rented
and never got around to watching
(if only   if only she'd insisted on a romance)

when the poem aims for romance
it leaves behind hickeys and groping
favours the architecture of desire
a house of skin and bone

when I write "husband" I sometimes mean
the kind I have
and other times the kind I won't:
the ones who claim never
to have picked a scab and enjoyed it
and the ones who punctuate
their own jokes with flatulence

(when I say "flatulence" I mean what I say)

when I write about the physical body
I try not to get too attached

for example   when I say "breast"
I mean it in its most useful form
and when I write of nakedness I want to hide
behind someone fully clothed

when I write "you" I mean you in the black shirt
with the comfortable shoes   you who feels all eyes
in the room riveted on your every breath and move
what will you say when you open your mouth?

when the words become lies and the lies
wear the names of people I know
I want to believe they are secretly proud
leave the room and page thinking
that poem is about me   she means me
I want her to mean me

Revelations, Age Eight

The number of the beast was enough
to scare anyone especially when Uncle Wayne preached
of European plans to tattoo the digit
666 on the forehead of every consumer

take the number and go to hell
or brave the tribulation as a true follower
starving in the end-times wasteland

I pictured me   my brother and mom
with bloated bellies   stick arms and legs
drinking mouthfuls of snow
foraging for rosehips and tree bark
desperate for the rapture
with my equally devout relatives
hollow-eyed cousins   gaunt aunts and uncles

and what would become of my father
who hadn't been to church in years
though he choked up Sundays at 4 P.M.
whenever Tommy Hunter sang the old hymns

those evenings he'd pull his harmonica
from the junk drawer
run his mouth over the hollow teeth
in a rusty version of "Jesus Loves Me"

his eternity my dilemma
knowing he couldn't go a day without his Export A's
knowing he'd believe the apocalypse a sham
would march on down to the bank or co-op or village office
wherever a guy had to go to get that beastly mark
and me quietly grateful for his lack of faith
selling him out for a can of mushroom soup
a box of crackers

together our family at the kitchen table
straddling the fault line
between paradise and damnation
my father's feet in the fire
the rest of us already eating the banquet

Calling the Miles

Morning's weary half-light
and somewhere down a logging road
my father in his silver Kenworth
calls the miles on his radio phone
counts the night-shift hours until home
a slow cigarette and a mug of rye and Coke

while my mother at the breakfast table reads to us
from her Bible thumbed to a chapter in Acts
my brother and I with our spoons
in steaming cream of wheat
listening to Saul and the blinding light
on the way to Damascus

      ✳

Wondering always what moment he chose to turn
away from the high German hymns
and evening prayer meetings
the whole family walking three miles in snow
and rain and hot summer dust
to sit in the church's straight-backed pews
men on one side   women on the other
their voices rising to touch in the air

what moment he named his own father God
the fist and sharp tongue whipping down
blood buckling under the weight of blood
and heaven's brand of righteousness swapped

for a pack of smokes tucked under his T-shirt sleeve
late night cruising down the town's main drag

❋

Sunday mornings he slips quarters
and round white mints into our pockets
when he drops us off at the church's front steps

Mom upstairs for her adult Bible class
and children lined up in the basement for choir
with Aunt Betty squeezing her accordion
to the tune of *Do Lord oh do Lord oh*
do remember me   way beyond the blue
our names on the perfect attendance chart
marked by a row of gold foil stars

and he waits the two hours in the back parking lot
radio tuned to the local country music station
windows rolled up tight and cigarette held low

by noon and the benediction's song
the car's interior holds a thin cloud of smoke
my father's eyes rimmed with red and watering

❋

Evenings my mother tunes in our living room
for the *Back to the Bible Hour*
sits with her knitting by the stereo speaker
the click of her needles' casting off
against the radio preacher's urgent faith

out in his shop my father sits on a thick block
of spruce by the wood stove's easy fire
peeling another label off a bottle of Royal Reserve
to press onto the side of his tool chest
already three and a half rows of these
paper maple leaves stuck to the metal
red on black and rimmed with gold

later he will come in smelling of smoke
forget to bend down over our pillows
to say good night   the familiarity of this ritual
bringing comfort and an invisible hand to pull the covers up
always his feet struggling at the steep
and sudden staircase   always his eyes
sad with night's tenderness

❀

Waiting for the miracle to come close
lift off the pages of the Gospels
like the blind man at Bethsaida
new eyes shaped from spit and clay
or the beggar by the gate called Beautiful
his useless legs now taking their first step
toward home   on my knees nightly
praying my father's revival   and for heaven's
shaft of smouldering light to bear down
in the darkness on the long and weary road

Tongues of Men and Angels

After church noon blazing over the town
"On the Wings of a Dove" plays on the car radio
and the river flows like the body of a giant fish
catching light in a prism of scales

sitting in the back seat of the car I watch
the window inhale the contrails of my father's smoke
wondering about those forbidden tongues of fire
the Holy Spirit a fearsome ghost hovering in the sanctuary

stories of how it could overtake you
turn your body into a dizzy vehicle for the Divine
hearing about *those holy rollers* and imagining
their bodies rolling down the aisles
the way my brother and I rolled down grass slopes
the momentum sending us into wild laughter

❉

I thought he was speaking Russian
the missionary's prayer a chain of eloquence
and rolling words that spun off his tongue
like circles of smoke
you could almost hold in your hand

I'd love to learn a language like that I said
speak with a tongue not my own

understand I thought he was speaking Russian
and was not afraid of the flamboyant tongue

understand I thought the laying-on of hands
was something done in the dark
two coming together out of need or desire
a different kind of consuming fire

❋

Are you interested in the inner workings of the mind?
a small man on my doorstep
clutching a clipboard and some books
yeah sure I say *the mind and memory   I'm curious*
maybe he's searching my neighbourhood
for signs of intelligence or someone like me
do you believe in a higher power?

I know the sacred head
taste the bread and wine
each Sunday morning
and tell him I'm aiming
myself toward heaven
and the bright journey
then say something
vague about holiness

＊

Trying to find words to explain the presence of God
when the tongue escapes into another room
packs up and leaves for a more articulate architecture

it was a prayer meeting
and something settled
like a heavy cloak on the heads
of those who came

one man hiding under his chair
unable to stand the weight
of so much grace

＊

Terrified at the thought of surrendering
control over my own mouth
making myself a loose-tongued fool
the jargon of holiness and the soul's wreckage
breaking to the surface
and the fear   the fear of loss
now you have it
now you don't

✳

Reasons to keep my mouth shut:

because silence is a dialect of nuances I'm longing to perfect
one kind of quiet always implying another

because of the irreversible law of regret

because a foot in the mouth is far more difficult
than a bird in the hand

because you scare me with these heady whisperings
half-prophecy   half-threat

✳

Come unto me
all you who are weary
and heavy-laden
and I will give you rest

I have this dream night after night
of lying on my bedroom floor
dressed in thick coat and boots
a scarf wrapping my throat
held down by the garment of heaviness
and I can't move for all this weight
the sheer exhaustion of my load

Come unto me and find rest
my yoke is easy
my burden light

❋

Listening from the back seat to my father's humming
his left hand resting on the car's open window

there is the radio's song and the bright river
the tongues of men and angels in my head

always that white dove rising
and coming down

Beautiful

Sunday morning and me age twelve
leaning into the vanity mirror
with a fresh palette of eye shadow
moonlight river blue and *dusky lilac mist*
the sponge-tip applicator
smooth across my lid
and I'm thinking *beautiful*
or at least wishing

but good looks don't run in the family
the way thick bones and cowlicks do
our peasant blood too practical
for beauty says my mother too busy
with the dirt and muscle of this world

and always tells like a lesson how she and her sisters
would parade their childhood kitchen
wild rose petals pressed between their lips
until their father one day caught them
with his Bible and the story of Jezebel
the ashes in the fireplace spotted
with wilted pink kisses
by the time he was through

later in the church foyer when Aunt Lavonne
leans over my shoulder   whispers
like a prayer meeting that
eye shadow attracts demons

it's warning enough to push me
into the basement washroom to scrub
my face in the sink before service
the thought of all that evil flying
at me with their brown pointed teeth
slick tongues and eyes

enough to send me confessing
during silent congregational prayer
when the pianist plays
"I Lay My Sins on Jesus"   that spotless lamb
who washes all my crimson stains

Lies

Strange laws that mothers make
to bind their children   proverbs
from the massive Bible waiting
on the bed stand like a belt
or wooden spoon

mine is the gift I've convinced
my daughter I possess   genetic
in the mothering code   the ability
to look into her and see the truth
like a fleck of sawdust in her eye

did you wash your hands   make your bed
fold and put away your clothes? I'll ask
and *yes* she'll say turning to look
out the window or down at her socks
enough for me to know my daughter
still believes the picture of the story angel
with its feathered quill inking each sin
into her book of days like a string of red *X*'s
by a teacher's mean pen

like my mother's sing-song proverb
be sure your sins will find you out
the omniscient cycloptic heart
bearing down on my guilt
until repentant on the bathroom floor
I'd pour out a bellyful of sins
a swear word mouthed at the bus stop
the fierce wish that I belonged
to my uncle and aunt instead of this family

what are you doing in there?
my mom would holler
and I'd flush and flush until
certain each sin had been erased
the old book burnt
a new gilt-edged volume
opened to its clean first page

so my daughter six years old
cannot tell a lie   carries in her head
a scribbling angel   pen poised
over its luminous paper sheaf
waiting for the tongue to fall

meanwhile I keep my gift
these mother eyes bent earthward
fastened to the ground

Origins

Cold basement where the furnace
never burned warm enough
and the turntable scratched its way
through a winter of Smith Corona typing-tutor records
I learned first how to roll the paper straight
into the typewriter's black carriage
set the margins and tab precisely
sit up straight with hands placed comfortably
at waist level on the keyboard

let's begin said the disembodied secretary
and we did with a s d f *space*; l k j *space*
the keys' thin metal necks like scrawny beaks
in their peck and scratch for food
line after line until my fingers
could find those letters in the dark
and still her omniscient voice drilled on

by February I'd clocked forty-five words per minute
punching out full sentences about *now* being
the time for all good men to come to the aid of their party
until the picture in my head wrote a long line
of truck drivers carrying birthday cakes balloons
and brightly wrapped packages to our front door
my father in his Tijuana sombrero leading the troop
with a thirty-ought-six propped over his shoulder
the story leaping out until the turntable's arm

slid its needle off the record's subtle warp
and the carriage return's silver *ding*
sang like a trumpet in my ear

the idea splitting open the basement dark
the night I slipped record #8 ("Numerals and Symbols")
back into its paper sleeve   sat blank and waiting
for the omniscient secretary with her slightly Midwest lilt
or someone's voice to ring through my head
tell me what to say over the empty page

like I'm ready even now sitting down at the screen
fingers slightly curved and comfortable on the keyboard
waiting for the sudden fuse   that bomb with its slow burn
to paradise   a different omniscience pouring in my ear
the word and the tongue flying up in flames

Proverbs

The tongue of the wise useth knowledge aright
but the mouth of fools poureth out foolishness . . .

verse upon verse and syllable by holy syllable
our words roll out like the careful
curves and cursive loops our teacher thumbtacks
on the corkboard wall of neatness

The eyes of the Lord are in every place
beholding the evil and the good . . .

a choir of grade seven girls in crisp white
blouses pressed and pleated skirts
a recitation of uniform virtue
on the chapel's well-lit stage

The tongue of the just is as choice silver
the heart of the wicked is of little worth . . .

in the monthly scripture memory concert
our congregation of parents clap and sigh *amen*
these daughters worth more than rubies
more than sacks full of gold
and my mother in the front row
mouthing *smile*   her flash cube
flaring in the sanctuary

The lips of the righteous feed many
but fools die for want of wisdom . . .

and I'm still burning guilty from this morning
at the end of the driveway waiting for the bus
with the public school girls when I told
my first dirty joke lifted from the women's
bathroom stall at the local curling club

The mouth of the righteous bringeth forth wisdom
but the perverse tongue shall be cut out . . .

all of them laughing when I mispronounced
the punchline   the male anatomy
coming out crooked and clearly off
and me   standing dumb at the end of the road
fresh skirt and blouse and spit-shone shoes
hair combed back in new barrettes
while together they laughed and
and clicked open their pocket mirrors
twisted up their tubes of drugstore lipstick
shaped their mouths into perfect round O's

Doxology

To him who is able to keep me from falling
the way I fell at age five down the chimney
of our half-built house   came to stumbling
in the skeleton outlines of basement walls
until the carpenter scooped me up
and carried me to my mother who stood
paralyzed in the strawberry patch

To him who is able to mend the broken places
like my collarbone floating loose
under the doctor's cold hands   my split forehead
draped with black cloth and sewn closed
by the careful nurse's stinging stitch

To him who is able to cover all shame
and naked embarrassment when on the way
home from the hospital my father insisted
on stopping at the neighbours' house
to show them this accident and me
wearing nothing but underwear
shivering in the front seat of the pickup
while George Jones and Tammy Wynette
crooned their country love on the radio
and the neighbours clucked their tongues
through the driver's-side window

To him who is able to present me faultless before the throne
and before the mirror where I stood daily
watching my two black eyes change
purple to green to jaundiced yellow
and fingering the notch in my crooked shoulder
the black thread in my swollen brow

To him who is able to trade ashes for beauty
carve from the cracked bone unearthly scrimshaw
lace light through the skin of the uneven scar

Acknowledgements

The author gratefully acknowledges the financial
assistance of the British Columbia Arts Council.

The poems "Disclaimer" and "Psalm of Thirst" appeared
in the anthology *Introductions: Poets Present Poets*
(Fitzhenry & Whiteside, 2001).

I would like to thank Lance, Amelia and the rest of the
family for their constant love and support, Patrick Friesen
for his advice and encouragement and Silas White for his
generosity.

This book is for Grandpa Shenk.